Eleanor Roosevelt

First Lady of the World

David Winner

**BLACKBIRCH™
PRESS**

THOMSON

GALE

San Diego • Detroit • New York • San Francisco • Cleveland
New Haven, Conn. • Waterville, Maine • London • Munich

For more information, contact
The Gale Group, Inc.
27500 Drake Rd.
Farmington Hills, MI 48331-3535
Or you can visit our Internet site at http://www.gale.com

Photo Credits: cover © CORBIS; pages 12, 16, 18, 19 26, 27 © The Bettman Archive; page 40 © Gamma; pages 4, 54 (below) © Ferry/Liaison; pages 48 (both), 50, 51 (both) © Robin Harris; pages 7, 10, 11, 20, 33, 38, 42, 55 © The Hulton Picture Company; pages 44-45 © Image Bank; page 15 © Keystone Press Agency; page 8 (above) © Magnum; page 54 (above) © Network Photographers, Sparham; pages 6, 13, 14, 17, 28, 37, 42, 47, 56 © Popperfoto; page 9 © Rex Features; pages 24, 25, 30 (both) 59 © Franklin D. Roosevelt Library; page 8 (below) © Frank Spooner Pictures

LIBRARY OF CONGRESS CATALOGING-IN-PUBLICATION DATA

Winner, David, 1956-
  Eleanor Roosevelt / by David Winner.
    p. cm. — (World peacemakers series)
Summary: A biography of Eleanor Roosevelt, a politician, writer, first lady, and humanitarian who was instrumental in drafting the United Nations' "Universal Declaration of Human Rights" and convincing member nations to adopt it. Includes bibliographical references and index.
  ISBN 1-56711-975-1 (hardback : alk. paper)
  1. Roosevelt, Eleanor, 1884-1962—Juvenile literature. 2. Presidents' spouses—United States—Biography—Juvenile literature. [1. Roosevelt, Eleanor, 1884-1962. 2. First ladies. 3. Women—Biography. 4. United Nations. General Assembly. Universal declaration of human rights.] I. Title. II. Series.

  E807.1.R48W475 2004
  973.917'092—dc21   2003005136

Contents

A victory for humanity

On the night of December 10, 1948, the Universal Declaration of Human Rights was adopted by forty-eight countries of the United Nations (UN). Its articles set out the fundamental rights of every human being on this planet—including freedom from arbitrary arrest, and the right to food, shelter, and health care. The acceptance of the declaration by the UN was a unique achievement, and its success was due to one shrewd woman more than anyone else—Eleanor Roosevelt.

For two years, she had worked ceaselessly as chairwoman of the committee that drafted the declaration, carefully steering a path through the minefield of conflicting national interests. One minute, she would have to soothe the feelings of an outraged Communist delegate; the next, she would have to convince her colleagues to work longer hours. As one delegate said, "She was exceedingly practical and tough, though in an outwardly dreamy and idealistic way."

Her task was not easy. The optimism and good feeling among the Allies that had arisen after the miseries and sufferings of World War II were under severe strain. Already the lines of future conflict were being drawn between the East and West—communism versus capitalism.

Roosevelt was not to be deterred, however. As a politician, writer, and vital partner to one of the greatest U.S. presidents, she had fought for improvement in the lives of people everywhere. She believed that an international agreement of human rights—set out in a way that the average person could understand—would contribute to that improvement. She wrote during the United Nations debate, "Hopes have been aroused in many people through the ages. But it has never been possible for the nations of the world to come together and try to work out in cooperation such principles as will make living more worthwhile for the average human being." Her creation of the right atmosphere for the adoption of the Universal Declaration of Human Rights was perhaps her greatest achievement—in a list of many.

Eleanor Roosevelt worked at the United Nations (pictured) and fought for human rights.

5

Roosevelt continued to attract crowds even when she was no longer in public office.

First lady of the world

In 1948, Eleanor Roosevelt was sixty-four and famous throughout the world. She had served as first lady of the United States—the title traditionally given to the wife of the president. As first lady, she had shown herself to be a uniquely compassionate, and energetic, woman at a time when the poor in her country were suffering as never before.

Roosevelt was a strong negotiator at the United Nations.

More than this, because her husband had a disability, she became virtually an assistant president. She toured the country and the world on Franklin D. Roosevelt's behalf, and also advised him and campaigned for him.

In particular, she became known as a friend of the poor and the oppressed, and she was always determined to investigate their needs and grievances for herself. One of the most popular magazine cartoons of the 1930s showed her deep in a coal mine: "Oh my God," says a miner, "it's Mrs. Roosevelt!"

Eleanor Roosevelt was no armchair intellectual who pontificated about the woes of the world from her wealthy home. Although the Roosevelts were famous and rich, she identified with ordinary people, their fears and their hopes—and she showed it. She would shake a hundred hands in a receiving line and still seem interested in everyone she met. She

Though the human rights declaration Eleanor Roosevelt worked so hard to achieve was useful, children are still orphaned (above) and killed (right) by governments seeking power.

could sign and send one hundred letters a day and give each a personal touch. Because she had several close African American friends and regularly visited a mining community, she could understand the suffering of African Americans and sympathize with the plight of unemployed coal miners.

In spite of her fame and popularity, Roosevelt despised power for its own sake. She took as much delight in conversations with ordinary people on buses and trains as she did in negotiations with presidents and prime ministers—or in winning a vital debate at the United Nations.

Privileged, but unhappy

Eleanor Roosevelt was born on October 11, 1884, into a world of elegant and prosperous gentility. The people her family knew owned smart townhouses in New York and large country mansions along the Hudson River. Black servants, governesses, and maids

Roosevelt spent her life trying to help victims of violent governments, such as these children in Argentina.

. . . .

"[Eleanor Roosevelt] would not accept that anyone should suffer because they were women or children or foreign or poor or stateless refugees. To her the world was truly one world, and all its inhabitants members of one family."

—Jean Monnet, founder of the European Community

. . . .

took care of her and her two younger brothers, and her parents frequented the balls and meetings of an exclusive and aristocratic East Coast society.

Only once did the young Eleanor ever question her privileged position. This was when, as a girl, she witnessed a half-starved man attempt to steal a woman's purse. The face of "that poor, haunted man" disturbed her for many months, but it would take two decades before she would begin to understand the man's desperation.

A double tragedy

Despite the Roosevelts' wealth, Eleanor's childhood was not a happy one. Her mother, Anna Hall, was a classic beauty and a star of New York society. Eleanor was awed by her mother's elegance. As a toddler she would stand solemnly in the doorway and wait for her mother to acknowledge her existence. For years, it hurt Eleanor to remember "the look in her eyes and . . . the tone in her voice as she said, 'Come in Granny.'" ("Granny" was her mother's cruel nickname for her.) For the rest of her life, Eleanor was left with a sense of personal ugliness. Then, when Eleanor was only eight years old, her mother died.

By contrast, the young girl adored her father, Elliott. He was, however, something of an alcoholic and a playboy, and was often banished from the household for months at a time by Eleanor's grandmother, with whom the children lived after their mother's death. Eleanor longed for his visits, but these grew more and more infrequent, until he, too, died, when she was ten. "I did so want," she wrote pathetically, "to see my father once more." This double tragedy left Eleanor with a sense of being abandoned and unloved.

At her grandmother's home, the family still lived in a world of social advantage, but there were also strict rules and limited horizons. Ideas about women's rights and freedoms were still in their infancy, and Eleanor learned that women were expected to take their place in society as virtuous and dutiful daughters, wives,

Eleanor was eight years old when her mother died.

and mothers. It was not until she was fifteen and she was sent to school in England, that she got her first taste of a different life.

Allenswood was a small school for girls on the outskirts of London, run by Mademoiselle Souvestre, a lively, energetic teacher. This unconventional headmistress, known as "Sou" to Eleanor, drew the sheltered, melancholy teenager out of her shell and made her think for herself. Souvestre taught her students that everyone had a responsibility to try to make the world a better place. She also quietly challenged many of the accepted political ideas of the day. She disapproved of both Great Britain's and the United States's colonial adventures. Might, she said, did not make right; the powerful nations of the world ought to allow the small countries of the world to run their own affairs. These ideas were quite new to Eleanor, who had never thought to criticize politics or public affairs.

Although life at Allenswood was strict and far from luxurious, Eleanor thrived on it. "This was the first time in my life that my fears left me," she later wrote.

Though her family was rich and she had many advantages, Eleanor was not a happy child.

"Attention and admiration were the things through all my childhood which I wanted, because I was made to feel so conscious of the fact that nothing about me would attract attention or would bring me admiration."

—Eleanor Roosevelt

This painting shows a group of poor children in New York City. Though she lived in the same city, young Eleanor was sheltered from such scenes of hunger and poverty by her family's wealth.

Social graces and physical beauty were unimportant here. Instead, the development of a critical mind and a willingness to help others were encouraged.

A first flowering

With her quick intelligence and natural kindness, Eleanor was soon well liked by both teachers and students. Her confidence grew by leaps and bounds. The discovery that she had a knack of making the shy girls feel "naturally at ease" was as important in this process as the discovery of new intellectual horizons.

It was at this time that Eleanor developed a fascination for foreign travel. Twice, she accompanied Souvestre on trips to France and Italy. There, she learned to cope on her own—to make the travel arrangements, and get out to see new places and meet new people. "It was one of the most momentous things that ever happened in my education," she later wrote. It also made her proficient in three foreign languages—French, Italian, and German—that were to be vitally important in her later diplomatic career.

It was with feelings of sadness for friends left behind and a creeping dread of the social whirl of New York—in which she would be expected to play her part—that Eleanor Roosevelt sailed back to her homeland. Eleanor did not find life easy when she returned to her grandmother's house in New York in 1902. Much of her hard-won self-confidence disappeared when she was confronted with the demands of New York high society, and she once more became awkward and inhibited. As was the custom for aristocratic girls of the time, she officially "came out," or entered society, at the Assembly Ball in New York in December 1902. "I do not think I quite realized at the time what utter agony it was going to be or I would never have had the courage to go." she wrote. "I knew I was the first girl in my mother's family who was not a belle, and though I never acknowledged it to anyone at the time, I was deeply ashamed." In fact, she was a girl with both grace and intelligence, and there was one person in particular who realized this.

Marriage

Before she had left for England, Eleanor had met Franklin Roosevelt—a distant cousin—at parties given by her uncle Theodore Roosevelt (then the president of the United States). Now they met again, and Franklin, a student at Harvard University, was bowled over by Eleanor's shy charm. He wooed her for months with letters and declarations of everlasting love. Finally, after a "never to be forgotten walk by the river" near Harvard, Eleanor agreed to marry him. Years later, she confided to a friend that Franklin said he hoped she would help him to make something of himself—for he was highly intelligent and had political ambitions. For Eleanor, the idea of marriage seemed the natural thing to do, and she was pleased "to be part of the stream of life."

Their wedding on March 17, 1905, was the social highlight of the year. President Theodore Roosevelt, gave away his twenty-year-old niece in front of an army of newspaper photographers and reporters.

Eleanor, at age fifteen, was kind, intelligent, and well liked.

In 1911, Roosevelt was mother to three children—Anna, James, and Elliott. A fourth child, Franklin Junior, died in 1909.

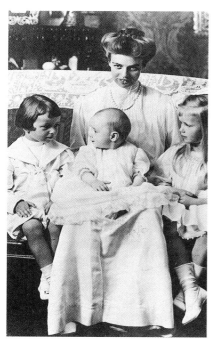

Less than domestic bliss

After the couple returned from their honeymoon in Europe, Roosevelt settled down to a life of domesticity. On the surface, her life seemed pleasant enough. The newlyweds moved into a house in New York that had been bought, furnished, and organized by Franklin's mother. Roosevelt had children in rapid succession—four in the first five years of her marriage. Like other wealthy young wives, she served on charity boards and attended classes in art, music, and literature. Yet somehow her life seemed frustrating and empty.

To begin with, she had to put up with her domineering mother-in-law, Sara Roosevelt, who took it upon herself to run Eleanor's household. Perhaps more important, like most well-bred young women of the time, Roosevelt had no idea how to bring up her children—after all, that was what the servants were for. Roosevelt felt guilty about this, but her attempts to do more as a mother often ended disastrously and left her feeling even more inadequate.

This feeling was accentuated when her third baby, Franklin Jr., died suddenly in November 1909. He was just seven months old. Roosevelt was in despair. It seemed to confirm something she had long suspected—she was a failure as a mother, too.

Meanwhile, Franklin had begun to take his first steps in what was to prove to be one of the most brilliant political careers in the history of the United States. In 1910, he ran as a Democratic candidate for the New York state legislature—and to everyone's surprise, he won. The couple moved to the state capital at Albany, and to Eleanor's immense relief, for the first time since the honeymoon, her mother-in-law did not accompany them.

Eleanor Roosevelt now set out to become a dutiful politician's wife. She researched issues her husband needed to know more about, attended speeches and committee meetings, and entertained the many people who visited their home. Even so, she still, in a sense, hid behind her sheltered position in society—she was not really interested in politics or the great issues of the day. She later wrote, "It was a wife's duty to be interested in whatever interested her husband, whether it was politics, books or a dish for dinner."

Indeed, she was quite shocked by some of the policies Franklin adopted. When he came out in support for women's right to vote, she wrote, "I had never given the question serious thought, for I took it for granted that men were superior creatures and knew more about politics than women did." It would take a number of traumatic jolts to shake Roosevelt out of her cozy existence and into the larger world.

World War I

One of the first of these shocks came when the United States entered World War I in 1917. The Roosevelts were then in Washington, D.C., where Franklin was assistant secretary of the navy—a job he

In the early 1900s, Franklin Roosevelt, Eleanor's husband and a member of the New York state legislature, supported a woman's right to vote. Eleanor was not yet the supporter of human rights that she later became, and was shocked by his view.

15

Eleanor Roosevelt volunteered during World War I and was jolted out of her sheltered lifestyle.

I WANT YOU
FOR U.S. ARMY
NEAREST RECRUITING STATION

. . . .

"The winter of 1917—18 wore away and remains to me a kaleidoscope of work and entertaining and home duties, so crowded that sometimes I wondered if I could live that way another day. Strength came, however, with the thought of Europe and a little sleep, and you could sleep, and you could always begin a new day."

—Eleanor Roosevelt

. . . .

loved. It was also one of the key positions in the administration of the U.S. war machine.

As in Europe, the war changed the face of the nation and made people question some of the old certainties of the social order. Within a year, 3.5 million men were in the armed services, and 2 million were sent overseas. In Washington, thousands of new administrators arrived, and uniformed men thronged the streets. The conflict also drew millions of women into roles to which they were unaccustomed. They became farmers, factory workers, and drivers, and also filled the more traditional jobs of canteen workers and nurses.

Roosevelt, too, wished to do something for the nation. She volunteered to work several days a week at the local canteen that was set up at the railroad

station to serve coffee and sandwiches to the troops. It was the first time since her earlier charity work that she went to work in the outside world.

Eleanor loved it. Despite the long hours, sometimes fourteen at a stretch, she found herself caught up in the laughter, the apprehensions, and the fears of the soldiers who were about to leave for the war. In some ways, it seemed so much more real than the elitist world of her upbringing.

Eleanor Roosevelt visited battlefields such as this one during World War I. These sights helped shape her lifelong dedication to world peace.

Turning point

The war was to influence Roosevelt in a much more serious way, however. In 1919, shortly after hostilities had ceased, she and Franklin visited the bloody battlefields of France. Touring the desolate and scarred landscape around St. Quintin, where so recently men had fought and died, made Eleanor feel physically sick. The experience made her a lifelong advocate of peace.

On her return to the United States, she was horrified by a visit to the naval hospital in Washington. There, she saw men whose minds had been unhinged by the horrors they had witnessed. The hospital was overcrowded and understaffed, and Roosevelt was determined to do something about it. She used her influence as the wife of a government official to make sure that an investigation was carried out. As a result, conditions did improve.

Eleanor Roosevelt had made a major breakthrough. She had come to realize that the human condition could be improved with positive action. No longer would she remain on the sidelines, a spectator to the injustices of the world.

Betrayed

There was another, more personal, reason why Roosevelt was forced to reassess her whole life and outlook. In 1918, while she sorted through her husband's luggage, she discovered some letters to Franklin from Lucy Mercer, her pretty young secretary. The letters revealed that Franklin and Lucy were lovers.

Although Eleanor had had her suspicions for some time, she was devastated. The betrayal brought back terrible memories of her childhood—loneliness, abandonment, and a belief in her own ugliness.

Eleanor offered Franklin a divorce, but such a separation would certainly have ruined his political career. After a few weeks, and with the help of friends and relatives, they managed to patch things up. In time, they became deeply affectionate partners in politics and in life. Even so, their marriage was never the same again.

These photographs show the severe poverty suffered by many New York City laborers in the early decades of the twentieth century. Roosevelt fought against injustices such as poor working conditions.

Eleanor never referred to Franklin's affair in public, and when she wrote her autobiography many years later, the subject was still too painful and personal for her to mention. To her friend and biographer, Joseph P. Lash, she confided, "The bottom dropped out of my own particular world and I faced myself, my surroundings, my world, honestly for the first time." Lash's verdict was that "It was fortunate for the United States and the world that [Eleanor and Franklin] stayed together, but she paid a price in forever searching for the 'oneness' that she considered the basis for a happy married life."

Lash also recalled that Roosevelt had, in a way, grown through the bitter experience: "A woman of strength and grace, she had been humbled. The taboos and blinders of social exclusiveness fell from her eyes." Later, Roosevelt wrote, "Somewhere along the line . . . we discover what we really are and then we make our real decision for which we are responsible." Roosevelt made her own decision and flung herself into her work for peace, civil rights, and women's causes.

The League of Nations

President Woodrow Wilson suggested that as part of the World War I peace settlement, an organization be set up to try to ensure future world peace. Consequently, in 1919, the League of Nations was established, and, although the United States refused to become a member, Franklin strongly supported its work. Franklin Roosevelt had done well during the war and was a respected figure in Washington. His influence as a politician was now so strong that he was nominated as the Democrats' candidate for vice president in the 1920 election.

It was at this point that fate took a negative turn for Franklin Roosevelt. The Democrats lost the election, and the League of Nations was doomed to failure—partly as a result of the United States's decision to turn its back on it. Most personally disastrous, however, was Franklin's battle with a dreaded disease.

In 1921, Eleanor's husband, Franklin, was paralyzed by polio. She encouraged him to continue his political career, and he went on to become president of the United States in 1932.

Polio

One day in 1921, Franklin was boating at his summer home on the island of Campobello, on the border between the United States and Canada. He felt a little ill, but, at first, he thought he just had a cold. The next day, he could not move his legs. For two weeks, his condition was wrongly diagnosed as a blood clot on the spine. Later, it became clear that he had polio, a serious disease that in those days often killed or crippled its victims. Franklin survived, but he never walked again without assistance.

Franklin Roosevelt's public life seemed to be over. No one could imagine a leader who could not walk. Former newspaperman Louis Howe, though, who was Eleanor and Franklin's closest friend and advisor, had other ideas. As Franklin battled through illness and then depression, Howe and Eleanor buoyed him up and eventually convinced him to return to politics—despite Franklin's mother's belief that any attempt to restart his career should be out of the question.

The crisis forced Eleanor Roosevelt to step out of the shadows and campaign on Franklin's behalf. In one way, she later wrote, the experience "made me stand on my own two feet."

"A highly capable politician"

Over the next few years, as Franklin came to terms with his disability, Eleanor took over as his political representative. She made speeches and expressed her own ideas. Even before Franklin's illness, she had begun to flex her political muscle with the League of Women Voters in New York and to edit a political newspaper. In this, as in everything else she ever turned her mind to, she worked phenomenally hard. Louis Howe coached her in political technique, and she began to develop her own impressive style as a public speaker. The *New York Times* observed that Eleanor was maturing into "a highly intelligent and capable politician."

"[Eleanor Roosevelt] functioned in a highly unorthodox way that defied all proper administrative charts. If she had been less tactful, less sensitive, if she had not always been careful to stay within the limits set by Franklin and to check with him to be sure that her activities were consistent with what he wanted done, her acts of compassion and her desire to be helpful could have degenerated into a scandal of meddlesomeness."

—Joseph P. Lash, from
Eleanor and Franklin

In her own right

Eleanor Roosevelt began to see politics as an excellent way to improve the world. She lobbied, with some success, for more influence and involvement by women in the Democratic Party. In 1923, she helped launch a nationwide competition to find a solution to world peace. One hundred thousand dollars—a truly colossal sum at the time—was offered to the person who came up with the best plan for U.S. cooperation in a peace plan, which would then be sent to Congress for approval. Twenty-two thousand plans came in, and the winning entry was eventually put before the public for approval in a national referendum. Despite the popularity of the contest, the referendum took almost a year to organize, and by the time voting took place, the public had lost interest.

Meanwhile, Eleanor had been just as busy helping Franklin recover his confidence. She told him, "I'm only being active till you can be again—it isn't such a great desire on my part to serve the world and I'll fall back into habits of sloth quite easily! Hurry up, for as you know my ever present sense of the uselessness of all things will overwhelm me sooner or later!"

Once again, Eleanor Roosevelt had sold herself short. No matter how she felt, though, there was no turning back. She had arrived as a national figure in her own right, and not merely as the niece of one president or the wife of a vice-presidential candidate. Franklin's return to fitness would accelerate the process of her transformation into a public figure.

The governor's wife

In 1928, seven years after he had been struck by polio, Franklin decided to run as the Democratic candidate for governor of New York. Few people expected him to win, and Eleanor put most of her efforts toward the campaign for the Democratic presidential candidate, Al Smith, in an election that would take place at the same time as Franklin's. In something of an upset, Smith lost, but Franklin won. Eleanor was so depressed about

....

"Her lack of pride and vanity and her sincere dedication to the public good inspired confidence in her fairness and judgment. By the time Franklin returned to political office some of the foremost women of the time, who had long been leaders in the struggle for women's rights, saw in Eleanor a new leader to whom they could pass on the torch."

—Joseph P. Lash, from *Eleanor and Franklin*

....

Smith's defeat by the Republican, Herbert Hoover, that she told a reporter she did not care about Franklin's election: "If the rest of the ticket didn't get in, what does it matter? . . . What difference can it make to me?" Over the next four years, however, Eleanor became used to life as the governor's wife.

The new role meant that she had to give up some of her activities. The public still was not ready for a politician's wife who was just as dynamic as her husband, and Franklin was not unhappy to portray Eleanor as more of a typical political wife than she actually was. Together, they visited hospitals, schools, and prisons, but Franklin thought it would look bad if Eleanor was seen to be too involved in politics in her own right.

Eleanor, therefore, directed her energies into new fields. She started a small furniture factory at her home in Val-Kill, a house she had had built near the Roosevelt mansion at Hyde Park. She also started to teach in Manhattan and continued to develop her skills as a public speaker and journalist.

"Black Thursday"

Meanwhile, a disaster was brewing. Investors in the New York Stock Exchange had been handling their money and investments recklessly for several years. Tens of millions of ordinary people had borrowed money to make more money in a spiral of increasingly risky speculative investments. As long as the market was on the rise, the problem remained hidden, and the country seemed to prosper. Then, however, on October 24, 1929—"Black Thursday"—the stock market crashed. The failure of one bank triggered a selling panic. Suddenly, no one wanted to buy stocks any more and everybody was desperate to sell. Sixteen million shares were dumped in a single day. In the stampede, thousands of companies went out of business. Railroads, banks, shops, and farms all failed on a terrifying scale. Millions of people lost their lives' savings almost overnight. Millions of others were thrown out of work. The United States

Both Eleanor and Franklin fought to help the many people who were out of work during the Great Depression.

After the stock market crash in 1929, people panicked and tried to withdraw their savings from banks.

plunged into its worst crisis of the century—and the shock waves spread to economies around the world.

The Great Depression

The years that followed the crash of the New York stock market were ones of misery for millions of Americans. The number of unemployed rose from 4 million in 1930 to almost 15 million in 1933. Families left their homes and farms in a desperate attempt to find work. Men who had once been rich sold fruit on street corners. People slept in cardboard boxes and foraged in the streets and trash dumps for their food. Some starved.

A visitor to New York described the "hardship, misery and degradation. . . . Times Square is packed with shabby, utterly dumb and apathetic looking men." The hero of a contemporary novel was one of these unemployed people: "The young man walks by himself through the crowd that thins into the night

streets; feet are tired from hours of walking . . . muscles ache for the knowledge of jobs, for the road-mender's pick and shovel—work!"

Everywhere across the United States, the story was the same. In his epic novel, *U.S.A.*, John Dos Passos wrote, "That winter, the situation of the miners in the Pittsburgh district got worse and worse. Evictions began. Families with little children were living in tents and in broken-down unheated tar-paper barracks."

Meanwhile, Herbert Hoover and his administration in Washington, D.C., seemed unable to do anything. The problem was that current economic thinking did not allow government interference to boost the economy and provide relief. The secretary of the treasury thought the slump would eventually right itself like a ship in a storm. He even thought the Great Depression would "urge the rottenness out of the system. People will work harder and enterprising men will pick up

Many people who lost their jobs during the depression became homeless. Camps like this one, called Hoovervilles, sprang up within major cities.

After he became president of the United States, Franklin Roosevelt helped poor Americans rebuild their lives with programs such as the National Recovery Plan.

the wrecks from less competent people."

Franklin Roosevelt attacked the Hoover administration's callous and wishful-thinking attitude in an angry speech in 1930: "Although the times call for quick and decisive action by the Federal Government, nothing happened but words. This was the time if ever when the government projects should have been accelerated and when public works should have been pushed to provide employment."

Eleanor, too, was appalled by the misery she saw all around her. She instructed her cook to prepare a constant supply of coffee and sandwiches, and she would send the unemployed people she met on the streets to her house to be fed. Private charity like this, however, clearly could not possibly remedy the current crisis entirely. Political decisions needed to be made.

President

In 1932, Franklin Delano Roosevelt—soon to be known universally as FDR—was elected president of the United States. In his famous inaugural speech he declared, "Let me assert my firm belief that the only thing we have to fear is fear itself."

In the first of a series of broadcasts that came to be called fireside chats, the president promised "action and action now in this dark hour of our national life." One writer commented, "For the first time in half a generation, the American people have elected a president who gives his fellow citizens the heartening picture of a joyous American working with a zest and smiling as though he had no misgivings for the future of the United States."

He might have added—"and with a wife and partner to match that zest!" Eleanor was working with FDR in their great push to beat the Great Depression.

The New Deal

The essence of the New Deal, which Franklin Roosevelt had promised the American people in the buildup to his election, was relief for the unemployed and government intervention to reverse economic decline—thus restoring confidence in American institutions and democracy. Unlike Hoover, Roosevelt accepted full government responsibility for all those who were out of work.

The president rapidly translated words into action. In an unprecedented swirl of activity between March and July 1933, referred to as the Hundred Days, he got the banks open again and unleashed a torrent of new laws and regulations to jump-start the economy back into action, to tackle poverty, and to rebuild the people's shattered confidence. The government spent massive amounts of money to create millions of new jobs on the land and in new industries and backed its assault on destitution with the establishment of a welfare system designed to protect the weakest members of society.

In all this, Roosevelt could rely on Eleanor's own high-octane brand of support and advice. FDR and

Franklin Roosevelt's administration spent millions of dollars to restart the economy. Under his "New Deal," men were given work that rebuilt their communities, such as this street repair project.

As president and first lady, Franklin and Eleanor Roosevelt were a powerful team. Eleanor was able to achieve many of her own goals, such as helping the poor, through Franklin's support.

Eleanor made a great team. He was a superb politician and policymaker. She, on the other hand, provided much of what one writer called "the conscience of the New Deal." She often inspired him and always pushed for more measures to help the poor and disadvantaged. She was also his most popular and effective representative and his physical link to much of the outside world. Where he could not go, because of his disability or the pressure on his time, he sent Eleanor.

First lady

At first, the ever-modest Eleanor had been extremely reluctant to move to the president's official residence, the White House. "I never wanted to be a president's wife, and I don't want it now," she was reported to have said immediately after FDR's election victory. As usual, though, her powerful sense of duty prevailed, and she soon saw the possibilities of her new position. "I truly believe that I understand what faces the great masses of people in the country today," she told a trade union audience. She and Franklin wanted to find a new cure for the despair and fear that had flooded through the country in the worst moments of the Great Depression: "We cannot live for ourselves alone. . . . As long as we are here on this earth we are all of us brothers, regardless of race, creed or color."

There had never been a first lady like her. Previous presidents' wives had stayed mainly in the background, entertaining foreign dignitaries and supervising domestic arrangements in the White House. Eleanor, by contrast, would throw herself into action with a sense of mission and energy.

Success

Almost immediately, Eleanor started to campaign against sweatshops, support soup kitchens, and speak out for the poor. She called for better salaries for teachers and made arguments against the use of children as factory workers.

In March 1933, eleven thousand unhappy veterans from World War I arrived in Washington to demand that the government pay them a bonus they had been promised. It was the second coming of the so-called Bonus Army. The first had been a year earlier, when Hoover had responded with violence, sending in soldiers with tanks, machine guns, bayonets, and tear gas to smash the protesters' camp and burn their tents. Roosevelt used a much more effective weapon: He sent Eleanor. To the horror of her security guards, she went into the middle of the violent protesters to discuss their grievances. In almost no time, she had won them over and was singing marching songs with them.

The visit to the veterans was typical of Franklin and Eleanor's strategy. When Franklin heard about a problem, he sent her to see it for herself. When she heard ideas or met someone she thought FDR should also hear or meet, she arranged it for him.

Sometimes it was hard for him to keep track of everything she did. On one occasion, FDR had sent her to investigate prison conditions and had then forgotten that he had done so. "Where's my Missus?" he asked her secretary. "She's in prison," came the reply. "I'm not surprised," the president remarked, "but what for?"

Failure

Security agents considered Eleanor's style very risky. They worried about what might happen if someone tried to assassinate her. Under pressure, she agreed to carry a gun in her car. With the typical relish she showed for a new challenge, she even became a pretty good shot, but insisted that she would never use the weapon on a person.

When disturbing reports came in about living conditions in depression-hit coal-mining communities in West Virginia, Eleanor went to investigate. She went down into the pits herself and visited dozens of miners' homes. She came back to Washington shocked. "There were some who did not know what it was to sit down at a table and eat a proper meal," she told Franklin. She launched a project that would help them by building a new town. This time, her instinct may have been caring, but the project turned

Above: Roosevelt was a supporter of black equality. She was a close friend of Mary McLeod Bethune (right), a leader in education and civil rights.

Right: Eleanor Roosevelt created informal garden parties for groups she felt needed attention and a boost in morale, such as these delinquent boys from a nearby school.

into a financial and practical disaster. The community failed, and her critics muttered darkly that the scheme was inspired by communism.

Upsetting the bigots

Eleanor Roosevelt was not afraid to take a stand on social issues during her years as first lady. One of her favorite causes was civil rights for black people, which were still a long way off despite the abolition of slavery more than seventy years earlier. Economic opportunities for most black people were almost nonexistent and racial segregation remained widespread, even in Washington.

In the Deep South, Roosevelt found herself at a meeting of the Southern Conference on Human Welfare in Alabama. The seating arrangements seemed to contradict the spirit of the event's title: The hall was neatly divided along racial lines. Whites sat on one side of the aisle, blacks on the other. To make her point about the need for desegregation, Roosevelt moved her chair into the middle of the aisle—between blacks and whites.

At a higher level, she successfully lobbied for a prominent black leader, Mary McLeod Bethune, to be appointed as director of Negro Affairs for the National Youth Administration. Roosevelt's public stand against racism earned her the hatred of bigots across the United States. Conservative newspapers wrote scornful pieces about her. Still, she refused to be intimidated. She politely ignored the insults. In May 1936, she organized a garden party in the grounds of the White House for the mainly black inmates of a training school for delinquent girls, where disease was rife and conditions miserable.

Reporters asked her why she was holding the party. All young people like to have a good time occasionally, she explained, and these youngsters were no different from any other young people. Roosevelt's efforts put Congress to shame, and led it to provide one hundred thousand dollars to improve conditions at the school. Racists—even those in her own party—were unmoved.

"What enchanted the press captivated the public. As First Lady, Eleanor's approach to people great and small remained as it had always been: direct and unaffected, full of curiosity and a desire to learn—and to teach."

—Joseph P. Lash, from *Eleanor and Franklin*

"She who had been anti-Semitic and prejudiced against 'darkies' had become the epitome of a concern that excluded no one from the circle of its compassion and love."

—Joseph P. Lash, from his preface to *Eleanor: The Years Alone*

31

When Roosevelt uncovered similarly dreadful conditions at a home for elderly black people, White House advisers tried to persuade her not to speak out about it. She swept their objections aside and said, "We should be ashamed. I was sickened. If that is the way we care for people who are not able to care for themselves, we are at a pretty low ebb of civilization."

Roosevelt made her feelings public again in 1939. The elitist conservative organization Daughters of the American Revolution (DAR) refused to allow the great African American opera singer Marian Anderson to perform in their Washington auditorium. Roosevelt, who was an honorary member of the group, stepped in at once and arranged for Anderson to sing instead for an audience of seventy-five thousand at the Lincoln Memorial. Eleanor Roosevelt had scored another point for civil rights and equality.

Roosevelt and the press

Roosevelt was also determined to change forever the image of women in public. She had noticed the way women were discriminated against in the newspaper world. Journalism was dominated by men, and the few women reporters who did have jobs were almost always kept away from political stories because politics was considered a masculine preserve. Roosevelt planned to break that pattern.

One of her first acts after she entered the White House had been to start a series of regular press conferences for women reporters only. Because newspapers wanted stories about Roosevelt, they had to give a lot more attention to their women reporters than before. Along with her daily column, "My Day," it was another way for Eleanor to reach out to an audience of American women who had never had such a star with whom they could identify.

No first lady had ever spoken out so publicly before on political issues—such as poverty and justice—or given so much help to ordinary people. Previous first ladies had generally been remote and unapproachable, but Roosevelt urged women to write

Roosevelt, shown here on the cover of Look *magazine, was able to speak directly to the public through her regular columns and articles.*

to her about their problems. The letters were usually about financial hardship or family troubles, and Roosevelt gave advice and sometimes even sent money. She earned money from writing articles and doing radio broadcasts and gave it to charity. It had never occurred to anyone that a president's wife could make an independent career for herself.

Roosevelt exuded independence and energy. As one writer put it, "To masses of American women, Mrs. Roosevelt stood alone as a symbol of unattainable prestige as well as a benevolent advocate and counselor who was readily accessible through the media." On the radio and in her column, Roosevelt urged people to volunteer for useful projects and to become politically active. "Do what you consider is the right and kind thing," she said.

Roosevelt and feminism

Eleanor Roosevelt also gave strong support to the idea that women had the right to work, a controversial proposition at the time. By modern standards, she would hardly be considered a radical feminist. When she was asked to consider a run for president in her own right, she laughed at the idea. Roosevelt claimed that women would be "too emotional" and were not as well trained as men for such a job. It was long before the likes of Margaret Thatcher, Indira Gandhi, or Golda Meir would prove her wrong. Despite her reluctance to become an elected official, as a hardworking, successful, and generous woman, Roosevelt became someone who inspired millions of women.

As her bulging mailbag testified, she was a powerful role model for millions. In her first year in the White House alone, she received 300,000 letters. Women all over the country adored her. To older women, as one observer put it, she seemed to be a "superwoman—a grandmother devoted to family, friends and worthy causes, presiding at the White House and flying around the country to give speeches." She was not only popular, she was also influential. Political analysts read her columns avidly for hints about what the president would do next.

Eleanor Roosevelt, columnist

Of course, not everyone adored or admired Roosevelt. Some considered her "My Day" column trite and tedious. The poison-penned but popular columnist Westbrook Pegler, who had once supported the Roosevelts but later made a living by attacking them, wrote a scathing parody of Eleanor's homely, earnest style.

Seen from the standpoint of today's cynical world, some of her views seem almost too sweet-natured, self-effacing, and virtuous to be true. In a monthly column in the *Ladies' Home Journal*, she asked people to send in questions for her to answer. Someone asked: Who were the greatest men of all time? The answer was "Christ. Aside from Him, it would be

> "Both by fate and personal will, Eleanor Roosevelt became the most important public woman of the twentieth century. As much as anyone, she represented that generation of women born in the late nineteenth century who moved from a Victorian role of dependency to a new assertion of self."
>
> —William H. Chafe, from his biographical sketch in *Without Precedent: The Life and Career of Eleanor Roosevelt*

hard to name any others, because for different reasons men have been outstanding and valuable at different times." As the greatest women she named nurse Florence Nightingale, scientist Marie Curie, and writer Harriet Beecher Stowe.

One letter asked Roosevelt how she would like to be remembered by history. She replied, "There is no accomplishment of mine that I think could possibly be important enough to be recorded, and I have no desire to be remembered except by the few people whom I love."

She was also asked more personal questions, such as whether she ever got lonely and how she cheered herself up. She answered "I can never remember being lonely, but if I feel depressed I go to work. Work is always an antidote to depression, and loneliness is just one of the manifestations of this frame of mind or state of soul which is the lot of all human beings."

Roosevelt also fielded uncontroversial questions on art, politics, marriage, and how to raise children. Whatever the subject, her views would be unshakably sensible, dignified, and cautiously modern. When asked what she thought about the new fashion in which women shook hands with men, Roosevelt said she was all for it: "It has never occurred to me not to do so [shake hands with men]. I was taught as a child that handshaking was an expression of friendliness, and I do not think of necessity it has to be limited to men."

She urged readers to study and read more often, to be more thoughtful to each other, and to confront and overcome their prejudices so they would be better able to respect people who were different from themselves. She wrote, "It is wise to teach children that intrinsically every human being has the same value before his Maker, but that the moment a child enters the world he is conditioned by his surroundings. There is inequality . . . therefore, we as individuals should always try to recognize the actual worth of a human being as such and work toward a world where every individual may have the chance to develop his abilities to the greatest possible extent."

"Nothing galvanized Eleanor into action more quickly than afflicted human beings in whom some spark of aspiration and hope still glowed. . . . She listened to the miners' wives and took their babies on her lap. She went into the hovels alongside of Scotts Run, one of the worst slums in the country, where mine tipples rusted and the gully that was used for cooking and washing water also ran with sewage."

—Joseph P. Lash, on Eleanor Roosevelt's visit to West Virginia, from *Eleanor and Franklin*

"I would rather die than submit to tyranny"

By the late 1930s, such caring ideas were menacingly out of fashion in large parts of Europe, where dictatorships were on the march and war loomed again. Although Eleanor Roosevelt had always believed passionately in the need for peace, she was not an absolute pacifist. Despite the revulsion she felt after World War I, she came to believe that when it came to ruthless enemies such as the Nazis, it might be best to stand up and fight back.

Traditionally, the United States had been a neutral country, and many Americans did not want to get involved in the coming European conflict. That was not Roosevelt's view. She said, "I am not neutral in feeling as I believe in democracy and the right of people to choose their own government without having it imposed on them by [Benito] Mussolini or [Adolf] Hitler." She said she would "rather die than submit to rule by Hitler or [Joseph] Stalin. The Nazis would have to be stopped by force, if all else failed."

"A date which will live in infamy"

The debate raged in the United States for the first two years of World War II. Franklin D. Roosevelt supported Great Britain morally and materially as it stood alone against Hitler during 1940 and most of 1941. Many other Americans, however, were not convinced that they would have to fight, at least not until December 7, 1941—the day Germany's ally, Japan, launched a surprise bombing attack on the U.S. fleet at Pearl Harbor, Hawaii.

In a speech to Congress, Franklin Roosevelt called the day of the attack "a date which will live in infamy." Overnight, support for U.S. involvement in the conflict had become almost unanimous. Franklin had chosen Eleanor as codirector of the Office of Civilian Defense, and in the first weeks of the war, she had a mountain of work to do. Her first task was to visit American cities that were panic stricken over fears of

a Japanese invasion. Her presence helped calm jangled nerves and set the pattern for much of her wartime effort. For the next three years, Eleanor worked day and night as a one-person morale booster for the Allies.

Her astonishing stamina, which had left reporters trailing in her wake during peacetime, was now stretched to its limits. One week, she would visit the rubble-strewn streets of bombed-out London, where she charmed blast victims, air raid wardens, and members of the royal family alike. The next week, she might make a visit to American soldiers in Australia. Everywhere she went, her impact provided a psychological boost. "You certainly have left golden footprints behind you," said British prime minister Winston Churchill, after Roosevelt made a trip to Great Britain in 1942. Roosevelt seemed to be everywhere—she almost seemed close enough to every war front to dodge the bullets. When British commandos launched

Although passionately committed to peace, Eleanor Roosevelt believed it was appropriate to fight back against enemies such as Adolf Hitler (second from right) and the Nazis.

Eleanor acted on behalf of Franklin during World War II. She visited troops on the front lines and viewed war damage.

a daring raid on German-held Dieppe, a cartoon appeared that showed Roosevelt in a dinghy alongside them, dictating her column for the next day's "My Day."

The tide turns

Eleanor Roosevelt never lost sight of the values for which the Allies had begun to fight the war. When she learned that Japanese Americans had been interned in camps after the attack on Pearl Harbor, she was brave enough to lodge a protest. She strongly believed that the internment was wrong, since there was no evidence that Japanese Americans would be disloyal to the country. It was an unpopular thing to do in the inflamed atmosphere of the time, but it showed that she would not muffle her commitment to decency and justice for the sake of a quiet life.

From 1943 on, the tide of war turned to the benefit of the Allies, and Franklin Roosevelt's thoughts turned to ways to establish a new world order after the war. As president in the 1930s, FDR had done much to put the idea of a society built on justice and greater civil and human rights before the American public. Now he tried to ensure that human rights would be one of the Allies' war aims.

Back in 1941, Germany had been close to winning the war. Hitler's armies had subjugated almost all of Europe and seemed close to defeating the Soviet Union. British leader Winston Churchill had understood that if the Nazis succeeded, civilization would be destroyed and replaced by the Nazis' racist society. "If we fail," Churchill said in a famous speech before the Battle of Britain, "then the whole world, including the United States, including all that we have known and cared for, will sink into the abyss of a new Dark Age, made more sinister and perhaps more protracted, by the lights of perverted science."

The United Nations

FDR had recognized the same mortal danger. Both he and Churchill were determined to do everything in their power to clearly put forward their alternative to the Nazis' plans for the future. In 1942, Roosevelt and Churchill had declared that British and American "faith in life, liberty, independence and religious freedom, and in the preservation of human rights and justice in their own lands as well as in other lands" would be given "form and substance and power through the . . . United Nations."

It was a noble promise. Plans for the creation of a United Nations started immediately, with the issue of human rights firmly on the agenda. When the war ended and the world recoiled in horror from the results of Nazi ideology—mountains of corpses in the death camps, cities reduced to rubble, and an exhausted continent in ruins—the people who had survived hoped fervently that the wartime vision of a just world peace would be put into practice. She did not yet know it, but much of that duty would fall to Eleanor Roosevelt.

"Eleanor received criticism for particular stands. . . . Her highly publicized travels drew out critics who were disturbed by the spectacle of a woman making a mark in the world. 'Why don't you buy yourself some stuff to knit with instead of using the army's gas to go on your pleasure trips. . . .' 'If you would stay home and make a home for your husband, it would be O.K.' Other citizens wrote Eleanor telling her to 'keep Franklin company (as a real good woman should do)' and 'tend to her knitting as an example for other women to follow.' She was characterized as a 'female-dictator who would advise her husband' and as a 'selfish, pleasure-loving woman.'"

—J. William T. Youngs, from *Eleanor Roosevelt: A Personal and Public Life*

Franklin Roosevelt and British leader Winston Churchill created the idea of the United Nations to ensure that scenes such as this one from a Nazi concentration camp never happened again.

FDR dies

On April 12, 1945, personal and national tragedy struck. Just a few weeks before the Nazi surrender, Franklin Delano Roosevelt died suddenly.

Eleanor, the nation, and the world were stunned. Millions of people reacted to the news with personal grief as if they had lost their own relative. Eleanor was desolate and felt that her own useful life had also ended. No one had ever given her a greater sense of security than Franklin did, she had once said. She wrote to a friend, "I am frightened. Who will take care of us now?" To a reporter she said sadly and simply, "The story is over."

Eleanor's story, however, was not over. In a sense, it had just begun. For the rest of her life, Eleanor Roosevelt, who had been the remarkable wife of a great president, became something very close to the conscience of her generation. She did this not in her own country alone: She became something very close to the voice of a common humanity.

Despite her grief, Roosevelt, at the age of sixty-one, began to pick up the pieces of her life. She resumed her "My Day" column; offered advice to the new president, Harry S. Truman, and other officials who asked for it; and began to plan for the future. "I shall hope to continue to do what I can to be useful, although without my husband's advice and guidance I feel very inadequate," she wrote. She hoped the new international organization that was taking shape—the United Nations—would live up to FDR's dreams. In fact, as Joseph P. Lash put it, "she now emerged as the principal champion and interpreter" of FDR's hopes and ideals.

United Nations delegate

The United Nations—FDR's dream—had begun to take on solid form. Like the ill-fated League of Nations before it, it was set up as an international arbiter of nations' grievances—through peaceful means, if possible. Unlike its predecessor, though, the UN counted both the United States and the Soviet Union as full members. Eight months after Franklin Roosevelt's death, Truman asked Eleanor Roosevelt to serve on the American delegation to the first meeting of the UN General Assembly in London. She was reluctant, since she had no formal diplomatic or parliamentary experience, but she agreed.

The experienced diplomats on the delegation, including a future secretary of state, John Foster Dulles, shared Roosevelt's doubts about how effective she might be. They saw to it that she was given a job where they thought she could do the least amount of harm. She was assigned to Committee III, which would deal with humanitarian, social, and cultural issues.

To the delegates' surprise, Committee III turned out to be the scene of some of the fiercest debates, and Roosevelt was soon in the middle of the hottest dispute of the General Assembly. After the war, the people of the world had hoped for peace, prosperity, and a chance to rebuild. Instead, rivalry between the United States and the Soviet Union plunged the world

Gas ovens were used by the Nazis during World War II to incinerate the bodies of people they killed because they regarded them as subhuman. Eleanor Roosevelt spoke out against Hitler and the Nazis.

"After Franklin Roosevelt's death, admirers as well as detractors had assumed—as she had herself—that Eleanor Roosevelt would gradually fade from public sight into 'a private and inconspicuous existence.' Yet of all of Roosevelt's associates, she had become more rather than less of a public eminence."

—Joseph P. Lash, from *Eleanor: The Years Alone*

World War II left millions of Europeans homeless. The United Nations tried to help these people.

straight into the tensions, fear, and rivalry of the Cold War. In 1946, Committee III was about to become one of the forums for this new tension.

Clash with Vyshinsky

More than a year after the war, more than a million people were stranded in refugee camps across Europe—mostly in Germany. These refugees were from the countries of Eastern Europe, such as Latvia, Poland, and Hungary, that had been occupied by the Soviets. The Soviets demanded that the refugees return to their homelands and face punishment. The refugees, though, had heard of mass executions in their former homelands and did not want to live under Communist rule.

After an exhausting round of difficult negotiations in Committee III, the issue was brought to the full meeting of the UN General Assembly. The Soviet delegate was Andrei Vyshinsky, the toughest opponent imaginable. The more experienced men in the U.S. delegation wanted to avoid a direct confrontation with him, so they pushed Eleanor Roosevelt forward as their representative.

Vyshinsky said that the displaced persons were using the refugee camps to make anti-Soviet propaganda and claimed that any refugees who did not want to go home must be "traitors, war criminals or collaborators." Roosevelt, who spoke without notes, made a passionate speech in which she argued that basic human rights would be broken by the forced repatriation of the refugees. After a fiery confrontation, Eleanor Roosevelt was judged to have won the debate, and the Soviets lost the vote.

A capacity for hard work

The quality of Roosevelt's performance had also struck a blow for feminism. Her male colleagues were suitably impressed. One admitted to her that he had been against her appointment at first, but now thought she was a fine representative. Delighted to have made her point, Roosevelt told a friend: "Against all odds the women inch forward. . . ."

Eleanor Roosevelt soon earned a reputation as the hardest working delegate at the United Nations and the most effective member of the U.S. team. She studied papers around the clock, attended meetings, and talked with everybody. She combined charm, warmth, and a fantastic capacity for hard work. Everyone respected and liked her.

"A task for which I am ill-equipped"

Following her success on Committee III, Eleanor Roosevelt was asked to be the U.S. representative on the UN commission to draft a Declaration of Human Rights for the world. This job would be a crucial element in the achievement of FDR's dream, and it turned out to be the most important role in Eleanor's life.

Roosevelt accepted the position—but again, she worried if she could do the job. She had long suffered from bouts of insecurity—a persistent feeling left over from her sense of abandonment as a child. She had not wanted to go to the United Nations in the first

"Before the Second World War there was no general international law on human rights. By and large, governments could still do as they wished with their citizens. Five years of war changed all that. Simply because of their race, people had been massacred, deported, tortured, their property confiscated and their children kidnapped. What the Declaration voiced was a determination that never again should people be so vulnerable to the frenzies of governments, and a recognition that there could never be a secure peace while governments were free to bully and massacre them."

—Caroline Moorehead, from the *Independent*

Flags from around the world fly outside the United Nations, where Roosevelt helped create a document that set international standards for human decency.

place. Now she worried—apparently in all seriousness—if, without a formal university education, she was really qualified. The task of writing a first draft of the new world bill of rights "may not seem so terrifying to my colleagues . . . all of whom are learned gentlemen. But to me it seems a task for which I am ill-equipped," she wrote.

The Economic and Social Council had chosen her to serve on the all-important commission, but it was the other members who unanimously chose her as their leader. Her great warmth and her understanding of ordinary people's needs would make her more useful than all the academics and intellectuals around her. She said, "I may be able to help them put into words the high thoughts which they can gather from past history and from the actuality of the contemporary situation, so that the average human being can understand and strive for the objectives set forth."

Roosevelt turned out to be a brilliant chairwoman: patient, hardworking, able to soothe the differences between the delegates. Without her, the process could never have worked. "I don't know of another human being in the whole wide world who could have done it," said a colleague later. "There wouldn't be a Declaration on Human Rights if she hadn't worked so hard at analyzing what every country and every delegate brought to the issues."

Working out the details

The commission members came from every corner of the globe, and their philosophical, religious, and ethical differences appeared at every turn. Line by line, word by word, month by month, Roosevelt steered them through the haggling over details. She was determined to find common ground.

Even the declaration's opening sentence, "All men are created equal," which was based on the opening sen-

"Some things I can take to the first meeting, a sincere desire to understand the problems of the rest of the world and our relationship to them; a real good-will for all the peoples throughout the world; a hope that I shall be able to build a sense of personal trust and friendship with my co-workers, for without that type of understanding our work would be doubly difficult."

—Eleanor Roosevelt, on her hopes for her work with the United Nations

tence of the U.S. Declaration of Independence, caused problems. The delegate from India pointed out that women should also be included, and another UN committee lobbied for the word "people" to be used instead of "men." The final compromise was "human beings."

No sooner was that difficulty sorted out than a Communist delegate objected to the word created, because that implied the presence of a God, and Communists did not believe in God. The committee agreed on "born free and equal" instead.

The great divide

Next, Roosevelt experienced the great divide between the West and the Third World in the emphasis placed on different human rights. The poorer nations were deeply committed to the rights that aimed at eradication of hunger, disease, illiteracy, and homelessness. To some of their governments it seemed almost irrelevant in comparison to fight for the rights of a few political prisoners.

Roosevelt's biggest challenge in the negotiations on the declaration involved the Soviet Union. Basically, "human rights" had a different meaning to Soviets and Westerners. In the West, "human rights" conjured up images of political persecution, imprisonment, and torture, and the Soviet gulags epitomized the lack of human rights. For Soviet delegates, on the other hand, "human rights" referred to people's right to employment, to medical help, to education, and to freedom from hunger. Viewed from the Soviet Union, Western unemployment, homelessness, and poverty were serious violations of rights. Despite reluctance from the United States and other Western delegates, Roosevelt was strongly influenced to include rights to employment, housing, and medical aid in the declaration.

On one issue there was to be no compromise, however: the clauses that covered freedom of the individual were not accepted by the Soviets. Roosevelt came out in favor of protecting the rights of individuals, whereas the Soviets claimed that the needs of the state were more crucial.

The paintings on the following pages were part of an exhibition to help people become more aware of the information in the Universal Declaration of Human Rights that Roosevelt helped create. A painting was made for each article of the declaration. Top: This painting represents the freedom, dignity, and equality discussed in ARTICLE 1. Bottom: ARTICLE 2 states that people should be treated equally regardless of differences in race, sex, religion, political opinion, or status of homeland.

ARTICLE 1

All human beings are born free and equal in dignity and rights. They are endowed with reason and conscience and should act toward one another in a spirit of sisterhood and brotherhood.

ARTICLE 2

Everyone is entitled to all the rights and freedoms set forth in this Declaration without dissection of any kind, such as race, color, sex, language, religion, political or other opinion, national or social origin, property, birth, or other status. Furthermore, no distinction shall be made on the basis of the political, jurisdictional, or international status of the country or territory to which a person belongs, whether it be independent, trust, non-selfgoverning, or under any other limitation of sovereignty.

On this point, Eleanor Roosevelt's patience was tested to its limits. Yet she refused to give up. "No amount of argument ever changes what your Russian delegate says or how he votes. It is the most exasperating thing in the world," she wrote. She added, though: "I have made up my mind that I am going through all the arguments just as though I didn't know at the time it would have no effect. If I have patience enough, in a year from now perhaps the Russians may come with a different attitude."

"The basic document of our times"

The declaration was one of the great documents of the century: a ringing prayer of hope for justice and dignity after an era when "disregard and contempt for human rights have resulted in barbarous acts which have outraged the conscience of mankind." Just two pages long, it set out the standards for basic human decency and provided a recipe for the abolition of tyranny and oppression. As one observer wrote, it was to become "the basic document of our times, the strongest, most stirring, most complete description ever of the rights of individuals and the duties of nations."

"Everyone has the right to freedom of thought, conscience and religion," declared one crucial article. "Everyone has the right to life, liberty and security of person," said another. The articles set out clearly the essential need for the rule of law, privacy, democracy, and education. The declaration acknowledged rights of culture, a healthy standard of living, and the rights to marry and found a family, as well as to work, to seek asylum from persecution, and to own property. Under the declaration, all people should also be able to move freely and to have a nationality. No one should be subjected to slavery or punishment. Everyone has the right to a fair trial, and to be protected against violations of fundamental human rights. According to the declaration, "All are equal before the law and are entitled without any discrimination to equal protection of the law."

ARTICLE 3

Everyone has the right to life, liberty, and security of person.

ARTICLE 4

No one shall be held in slavery or servitude; slavery and the slave trade shall be prohibited in all their forms.

ARTICLE 5

No one shall be subjected to torture or to cruel, inhuman, or degrading treatment or punishment.

ARTICLE 6

Everyone has the right to recognition everywhere as a person before the law.

ARTICLE 9

No one shall be subject to arbitrary arrest, detention, or exile.

ARTICLE 10

Everyone is entitled in full equality to a fair and public hearing by an independent and impartial tribunal, in the determination of their rights and obligations and of any criminal charge against them.

ARTICLE 11

(1) Everyone charged with a penal offence has the right to be presumed innocent until proved guilty according to law in a public trial at which one has had all the guarantees necessary for one's defense.

(2) No one shall be held guilty of any penal offence on account of any act or omission which did not constitute a penal offence, under national or international law, at the time when it was committed. Nor shall a heavier penalty be imposed than the one that was applicable at the time the penal offence was committed.

The declaration is adopted

In 1948, Eleanor Roosevelt spoke to the General Assembly of the United Nations in Paris before the vote to accept the declaration. This would be the last great hurdle; she knew it was a historic moment. "We stand today at the threshold of a great event, both in the life of the United Nations and in the life of mankind," she said. "This Universal Declaration of Human Rights may well become the international Magna Carta of all men everywhere. We hope its proclamation by the General Assembly will be an event comparable to the proclamation of the declaration of the rights of man by the French people in 1789, the adoption of the Bill of Rights by the people of the United States and the adoption of comparable declarations at different times in different countries.

"At a time when there are so many issues on which we find it difficult to reach a common basis of agreement, it is a significant fact that fifty-eight states have found such a large measure of agreement in the complex field of human rights. This must be taken as testimony of our common aspiration first voiced in the Charter of the United Nations 'to lift men everywhere to a higher standard of life and to a greater enjoyment of freedom.'"

To Eleanor Roosevelt's dismay, the full General Assembly did not vote on the document at once, but insisted on another debate that would examine the document line by line. It was an ordeal, and given the vehemence of Soviet attacks on the wording, she feared the declaration might be derailed.

On December 10, 1948, in the Palais de Chaillot, the Assembly finally voted on the declaration. The Soviet Union was still unhappy about it, but in the end, the Soviets and their Eastern bloc allies merely decided to abstain rather than vote against the declaration. Only two other countries joined the Soviets— Saudi Arabia, whose delegate thought his king would not approve of the idea that people could change their religion, and South Africa. The declaration was passed with forty-eight votes for, eight abstentions, and two countries absent.

ARTICLE 16

(1) Men and women of full age, without any limitation due to race, nationality or religion, have the right to marry and to found a family. They are entitled to equal rights as to marriage, during marriage and its dissolution.

(2) Marriage shall be entered into only with the free and full consent of the intending spouses.

(3) The family is the natural and fundamental group unit of society and is entitled to protection by society and the State.

ARTICLE 18

Everyone has the right to freedom of thought, conscience and religion; this right includes freedom to change their religion or belief, and freedom, either alone or in community with others and in public or private, to manifest their religion or belief in teaching practice, worship, and observance.

Opposite: ARTICLE 11 *states that a person has the right to be thought innocent until proved guilty. Above:* ARTICLE 16 *discusses men's and women's rights when marrying and starting a family. Race, nationality, and religion may not limit their rights. Left: Everyone has the right to freedom of thought, conscience, and religion under* ARTICLE 18.

Only the first step

There was an undeniable excitement about the passage of such a beautifully worded resolution in the ultimate international forum. Roosevelt, however, now sixty-four years old, always knew that the declaration would be no use to anyone unless it was put into practice in a way that might help every person on the planet.

Ten years later, in 1958, she wrote, "Where, after all, do universal human rights begin? In small places, close to home—so close and so small that they cannot be seen on any maps of the world. Yet they are the world of the individual persons; the neighborhood he lives in; the school or college he attends; the factory, farm or office where he works. Such are the places where every man, woman and child seeks equal justice, equal opportunity, equal dignity without discrimination. Unless these rights have meaning there, they have little meaning anywhere. Without concerned citizen action to uphold them close to home, we shall look in vain for progress in the larger world."

Inside the United Nations, in the years that followed, progress continued steadily. In 1966, the UN adopted two covenants on economic, social, civil and political rights, which would complete the International Bill of Human Rights. In 1976, the whole bill finally acquired the status of international law. There were other later covenants that outlawed genocide and torture, as well as the creation of a permanent UN Commission on Human Rights and human rights commissions in Europe and the United States. In November 1989, the UN adopted a "Convention on the Rights of the Child."

Human rights abuses

Many governments have failed to live up to the standards of the declaration. Indeed, some—such as Suharto's Indonesia in the 1960s, Chile, Argentina, El Salvador, Idi Amin's Uganda in the 1970s, and Saddam Hussein's Iraq—have tortured, murdered, and tyrannized their own people while they continued to pay lip service to UN human rights principles.

Yet the urgent moral and practical message of Eleanor Roosevelt's Human Rights Declaration has changed the world for the better. Its message has filtered out into the political cultures of the world, and as the years go by, its influence increases. In many countries, individual citizens can now seek protection and justice under the principles of the UN Declaration of Human Rights. They can go to court in their own land or through international bodies such as the European Court of Human Rights.

In areas where the United Nations has failed to monitor or protest human rights abuses, independent organizations have emerged to do that work and have grown steadily in strength and influence. One of these is Amnesty International, founded by the British lawyer Peter Benenson in 1961.

Ahead of her time

In her passionate belief in the vital importance of human rights, Eleanor Roosevelt was decades ahead of her time. Thanks in large part to her work, the issue is now right at the top of the international political agenda. In the 1940s, countries accused of human rights crimes would hide behind the excuse that foreigners should not interfere in their country's domestic affairs. The climate of world opinion has changed radically, however. Many people now believe what Eleanor always believed—that common humanity links everyone in the world. Now, in the twenty-first century, there are signs that the days of tyranny in many parts of the world are coming to an end, thanks to great popular uprisings fueled, in part, by the demand for democracy and human rights.

In 1989, the sources of inspiration for the successful peaceful revolutionaries of Romania, Czechoslovakia, and Poland, and of the murdered students and workers of Tiananmen Square in China, were many and varied. So were they for the people of the Philippines who overthrew the tyrannical government of Ferdinand Marcos in 1986. The legacy of Eleanor Roosevelt and the other great human rights leaders certainly played their part in all those countries.

"[The Declaration has] turned out to be more important than anyone realized. It's been invoked so many times that it's now recognized as part of the customary law of nations."

—John Humphreys, author of the first draft of the Universal Declaration of Human Rights

"Forty years ago, the governments of the United Nations made a historic promise to the world: They proclaimed, for the first time in history, that all human beings would be recognized as free and equal in dignity and rights. This was the promise of the Universal Declaration of Human Rights. . . . That promise has not been kept."

—Franca Sciuto, Amnesty International

(Above) The human rights declaration tries to protect people who have committed no crime, but have opposed their government, such as this Cuban prisoner.

The declaration also has clauses that cover racial prejudice and persecution. In the United States, the Ku Klux Klan (right) still expresses its racial views through cross burnings.

Around the world, Eleanor Roosevelt continued to be almost universally loved and admired. The warmth of people's support for her pleas for peace and understanding showed that she struck a deep chord with ordinary people. Wherever she went, she was met by crowds of admirers. Her idealism and optimism were not shared by governments, though.

The passage of the Declaration of Human Rights, was meant to be only the first step in a series of international statements and acts of legislation designed to outlaw abuses of human rights all over the world. In particular, more detailed covenants on human rights, which moved more slowly through the UN system, were designed to make sure governments met their human rights obligations to their people. This made many governments nervous—governments are not

Mass graves, like this one in Cambodia, show that not all countries that signed the declaration follow its rulings.

Roosevelt spoke against Senator Joseph McCarthy (pictured). The methods McCarthy used to search for Communists in the 1950s went against Roosevelt's beliefs in human freedoms and rights.

• •

"I think I must have a good deal of my uncle Theodore Roosevelt in me because I enjoy a good fight and I could not, at any age, really be contented to take my place in a warm corner by the fireside and simply look on."

—Eleanor Roosevelt

• •

usually happy when they have to give up power in any area. In particular, Roosevelt's own government was very cautious about the idea. "If we are unwilling to enter into a treaty on human rights we are putting ourselves in the same position as is the USSR," she warned in her newspaper column.

The United States turns its back on human rights

In 1952, the situation deteriorated. The conservative former general and war hero Dwight D. Eisenhower won the election and replaced Truman as president. He strongly opposed making the UN covenant binding on the United States. So, too, did his new secretary of state, John Foster Dulles, who had been one of Eleanor Roosevelt's UN colleagues a few years earlier, but had since swung to the political right. One of Eisenhower's first moves was to accept Eleanor Roosevelt's resignation from her job at the UN. Shortly after, he decided that the United States would no longer take an active part in the drafting of human rights covenants and would refuse to ratify any such covenant.

Roosevelt was shocked. She said, "We have sold out to the Brickers [another leading right wing politician] and the McCarthys. It is a sorry day for the honor and good faith of the present Administration in relation to our interest in human rights and freedoms of people throughout the world. We use high-sounding phrases but we are afraid . . . our statesmen should feel somewhat embarrassed."

A private citizen again

Eisenhower's decision to accept Eleanor Roosevelt's resignation from the United Nations seemed strange to many. Given Roosevelt's reputation and her role in steering the UN through some of its finest decisions, it was a sad moment for the United States and the world.

Eleanor Roosevelt seemed hardly to mind, though. In fact, she was pleased not to have to represent a policy of which she no longer approved. In any case, she did not need titles or official jobs. She had become a world figure in her own right.

She refused to give up her commitment to human rights and the United Nations. She was now sixty-eight years old, but she immediately volunteered her services to the American Association for the United Nations and launched into a new career as a writer, broadcaster, and unofficial U.S. ambassador to the world.

Eleanor Roosevelt continued to pour her legendary talents into work she believed would help others. She was willing to go anywhere and do anything if she believed she could be of use to solve a local or world problem. So, in 1957, when she was given a chance to interview the mercurial Soviet leader Nikita Khrushchev, she jumped at the chance.

Despite—or rather because of—the Cold War, Eleanor Roosevelt was convinced about the vital need to keep both sides talking. Relations between the United States and Soviet Union were deeply frozen, so the interview was of world importance. The conversation was like a discussion between two world leaders rather than a conventional interview. The session lasted two and a half hours and covered the most urgent issues of the day: the Cold War, the nuclear arms race, and the bitter Middle East conflict, in which the United States had sided with Israel and the Soviets backed the Arabs. Roosevelt and Khrushchev also discussed Soviet mistreatment of its own Jews.

When the talk was over, Roosevelt joined Khrushchev and his family for a meal. "Can I tell our newspapers that we had a friendly conversation?" Khrushchev asked as she left. "You can say we had a friendly conversation, but that we differ," said Roosevelt. "At least we didn't shoot each other!" laughed the Soviet leader.

"During a normal week, Eleanor received a hundred requests for public appearances. She had to decline most, but those she accepted kept her busy with as many as three or four appearances a day. Eleanor began one spring morning with a breakfast conference at Bryn Mawr, took a train from Philadelphia to New York for a fundraising luncheon for a boys' school, drove to Poughkeepsie to deliver a late-afternoon talk at Vassar on the United Nations, went home to Hyde Park for a quick dinner, and returned in the evening to Poughkeepsie to attend a Girl Scout pow-wow. A good day's work."

—J. William T. Youngs, from *Eleanor Roosevelt: A Personal and Public Life*

"Life was meant to be lived"

In her late sixties and early seventies, Eleanor Roosevelt's travels around the world took her to places few young people had the energy to visit. Everywhere she went she was regarded as a world leader—and she was often mobbed by crowds of admirers. She went to Yugoslavia and was impressed by its Communist and former partisan leader, Marshal Tito. In Japan, she wondered aloud about what appeared to her to be a subservient role for Japanese women, and paid a visit to the city of Hiroshima, on which the United States had dropped an atomic bomb at the end of World War II. She visited Israel and other parts of the Middle East, and went to India and met its prime minister, Jawaharlal Nehru. Throughout her travels, she spread a message of warmth and stressed the need for peace.

By now, friends and family thought Eleanor should start to slow down. She could no more contemplate a quiet retirement, however, than think of voting Republican. She scoffed at the idea: "I could not, at any age, be content to take my place in a corner by the fireside and simply look on. Life was meant to be lived. Curiosity must be kept alive. One must never, for whatever reason, turn his back on life."

Back to the United Nations

At home, her newspaper column was still widely read. She had her own pioneering talk show on television, which boasted Albert Einstein as one of its guests. At the age of seventy-five, she took on a new job as a visiting lecturer at Brandeis University. She said, "When you cease to make a contribution you begin to die. Therefore I think it a necessity to be doing something which you feel is helpful in order to grow old gracefully and contentedly." By 1961, Eleanor Roosevelt still regularly topped the polls as America's "most admired woman" and was viewed by many almost as a best-loved aunt or grandmother.

That year, John F. Kennedy became president and he appointed her as a delegate to the United Nations

once again. When she arrived to take her seat, the delegates of all the other nations rose and gave her a standing ovation. This had never happened to her—or any other UN delegate—before, and it was one of her proudest moments.

Failing Health

Time was catching up with her, however. This time at the UN, she barely had enough energy to sit and watch the proceedings. Her health had begun to fail. In 1962, her close friend, Dr. David Gurewitsch, diagnosed her as suffering from a rare blood disease. She went into the hospital for a blood transfusion, but hated the humiliations of terminal illness. She seemed to make up her mind that she wanted to die as she had lived—with dignity.

Eleanor Roosevelt died on November 7, 1962, at the age of seventy-eight, and was buried in the rose garden at Hyde Park beside her husband. Tributes flooded in from world leaders, and she was mourned and remembered by ordinary people everywhere.

No epitaph would quite catch the sense of awe and love she evoked as perfectly as a cartoon published in a St. Louis newspaper a few days after her death. In it, a group of angels sits expectantly on the fluffy white clouds of heaven, as thousands of people on Earth had waited over the years to greet Eleanor Roosevelt on her travels. The face of one angel glows with sudden recognition and he simply says: "It's HER!"

Glossary

Allies, The: In World War I, the twenty-three countries that joined together to oppose Germany, Austria-Hungary, Turkey, and Bulgaria. In World War II, the forty-nine countries that joined together to oppose Germany, Italy, and Japan. The World War II Allies were the founding members of the United Nations.

Bloc: A group of people, parties, or nations united by a common interest.

Cold War: The period of tension, suspicion, and competition (especially militarily), which started after World War II, between the Soviet Union and the West.

Communism: A political system based on the ideal of communal, rather than private, ownership. Under communism, wealth is redistributed so that, in theory, distinctions based on class and money disappear. Instead, all members of society work according to their ability and receive benefits according to their needs.

Congress: The national lawmaking body of the United States. It is made up of two houses—the Senate and the House of Representatives.

Covenant: A formal agreement.

Democracy: Government by the people, either directly or, more commonly, through elected representatives. Also, a nation that is governed in this way.

Democrat: In the United States, a member of the Democratic Party, one of the two major political parties in the country. Today, the Democratic Party is considered the party of the working person.

European Court of Human Rights: The court was set up on September 3, 1958, to pass judgment on violations of the 1950 European Convention for the Protection of Human Rights. The court sits in Strasbourg, France.

Fascist: A general name given to anyone with extreme right wing, antidemocratic ideals. The original Fascists were led by Benito Mussolini.

Genocide: The deliberate extermination of a group or race of people. Genocide was outlawed in 1976 under the United Nations International Bill of Human Rights.

Hitler, Adolf (1889–1945): Born in Austria, he became leader of the Nazi Party in Germany. He became dictator of Germany in 1934 and started World War II in 1939 when he ordered the invasion of Poland.

League of Nations: An international organization set up at the end of World War I to try to ensure future world peace. It failed because member nations refused to put international interests before national interests. It did not survive World War II, and in 1945, it was succeeded by the United Nations.

Mussolini, Benito (1883–1945): Founder and leader of the Fascist Party, he came to power in Italy in 1922. From 1925, he ran the country as a dictatorship. Mussolini took Italy into World War II on Hitler's side in 1940.

Nazi: A member of the National Socialist German Workers' Party, which was founded in Germany in 1919 and came to power in 1933 under Adolf Hitler. The Nazi Party's ideology included control of the economy by the state, hatred of the Jews, and racial superiority.

Polio: Short for poliomyelitis. An infectious viral disease that attacks the brain and spinal cord, resulting, in severe cases, in permanent paralysis.

Propaganda: Information spread to influence people to support an idea or belief. Usually, such information is biased and misleading.

Racism: The belief that some races are superior to others. This allows people from one race to treat people from another race badly and often leads to segregation.

Refugee: Someone who seeks shelter, usually in another country, from war, persecution, or natural disaster.

Republican: In the United States, a member of the Republican Party, one of the two major political parties in the country. The Republican Party was formed in 1854 to oppose slavery and is often identified with business interests.

Segregation: The separation of one group of people from another, usually black people from white people. Under such a system, separate facilities are provided for each group, but usually those for black people are inferior to those for white people.

Senate: In the United States, the upper house of Congress. The Senate consists of one hundred members, called Senators.

Stalin, Joseph (1897–1953): The ruler of the Soviet Union from 1928 to 1953. In the 1930s, he ordered the murder of all his political opponents and rivals.

Tyranny: The unjust and cruel use of absolute power.

United Nations (UN): An international organization of countries to promote international security, peace, and cooperation. It was established in 1945 as a successor to the League of Nations and has its headquarters in New York.

Universal Declaration of Human Rights: Adopted in 1948 by the United Nations, the declaration details a number of economic, cultural, and political rights to which every living person is entitled. These rights include the right to life, liberty, education, freedom of movement, and equality before the law.

Important Dates

1884	October 11: Anna Eleanor Roosevelt is born in New York City. Throughout her life, she would be known as Eleanor Roosevelt.
1899	Eleanor, age fifteen, goes to Allenswood, a finishing school in England.
1902	Returns to the United States.
1905	March 17: Marries a distant cousin, Franklin Delano Roosevelt (FDR).
1906	May 3: The first of the Roosevelts' six children is born.
1909	The Roosevelts' third child, Franklin, dies suddenly at seven months old.
1914	World War I breaks out and continues until 1918. The United States joins the war in 1917, and Eleanor becomes deeply involved in war work.
1920	The League of Nations is established in Geneva, Switzerland. Eleanor Roosevelt joins the League of Women Voters.
1921	August: FDR contracts polio and is paralyzed.
1923	July: Eleanor Roosevelt serves on the committee for the controversial Bok Award—a competition to find a solution to world peace.
1927	With Marion Dickerman, Eleanor Roosevelt buys the Todhunter School in New York City, where she teaches drama, literature, and American history.
1928	FDR becomes governor of New York. Eleanor acts as his representative and becomes more involved in politics.
1932	FDR becomes president of the United States. As first lady, Eleanor Roosevelt works for women's rights, social issues, and world peace.
1933	Eleanor Roosevelt launches the National Youth Administration, a scheme to provide training and jobs for young people during the depression. September: Eleanor becomes involved in an unsuccessful project to help coal-mining communities in West Virginia.
1935	December 31: Eleanor Roosevelt's first "My Day" column is published.
1939	World War II breaks out and continues until 1945.
1941	The United States enters the war. Eleanor Roosevelt helps the war effort by raising money, knitting, and visiting the troops.
1945	April 12: Franklin Delano Roosevelt dies.
	The United Nations is formed.
	President Truman asks Eleanor Roosevelt, age sixty-one, to be a delegate at the first meetings of the United Nations in London. She is assigned to Committee III, which deals with social, cultural, and humanitarian issues.
1946	Eleanor Roosevelt is appointed chair of the commission set up to establish a permanent Human Rights Commission.
1947	January: The eighteen-nation Human Rights Commission holds its first plenary session. Eleanor Roosevelt is appointed to serve as the U.S. representative for four years. She is also appointed chair of the commission.
1948	December 10: The Universal Declaration of Human Rights is adopted by the United Nations.

1952	Eleanor Roosevelt visits India, Pakistan, and the Middle East.
	Dwight D. Eisenhower is elected president. He fails to reappoint Eleanor when she resigns from the United Nations Human Rights Commission.
1953	January: Eleanor Roosevelt becomes an educational volunteer with the American Association for the United Nations.
	May: Eleanor Roosevelt visits Japan, Hong Kong, and Yugoslavia.
1957	Eleanor Roosevelt, age seventy-three, visits the Soviet Union and meets Soviet leader Nikita Khrushchev.
1959	Eleanor Roosevelt becomes a visiting lecturer at Brandeis University.
1961	March: John F. Kennedy appoints Eleanor Roosevelt, age seventy-six, to serve on the U.S. delegation to the Special Session of the United Nations General Assembly.
1962	November 7: Eleanor Roosevelt dies at age seventy-eight.

"It isn't enough to talk about peace. One must believe in it. And it isn't enough to believe in it. One must work at it."

Eleanor Roosevelt

"If civilization is to survive, we must cultivate the science of human relationships—the ability of all people of all kinds to live together and work together in the same world, at peace."

Eleanor Roosevelt

"Many of us have fixed ideas of what we think our own country and the various other countries of the world should do, but if we rigidly adhere, each to our own point of view, we will progress not at all. We should talk together with open minds and grasp anything which is a step forward; not hold out for our particular, ultimate panacea."

Eleanor Roosevelt, from a speech at a meeting of women's clubs in 1925

Index